The Sky
Is Not
The Limit

1st Edition 1996
Reprinted 1997

WITHERBY

PUBLISHERS

ISBN 1 85609 103 1

Published and Printed by:
Witherby & Co. Ltd.
32-36 Aylesbury Street, London EC1R 0ET
Tel No: 0171-251 5341   Fax No: 0171-251 1296

British Library Cataloguing in Publication Data
Kilminster, Malcolm
The Sky in Not the Limit – 1st Ed.
1. Title
ISBN 1 85609 103 1

The Sky
Is Not
The Limit

A plain English guide to

setting and getting your goals

by

Malcolm Kilminster

- Use your potential
- Change your future
- Anything is possible

iii

iv

Preface

The Sky is Not the Limit

A personal growth guide to creating
your own future

I don't remember much about my childhood. I only remember that I seemed happy and on leaving school with 2 'O' levels and a girlfriend, seemed destined to do whatever came along. I was certainly aimless, and can now thank my father for enrolling me into the Royal Air Force, and thus, by accident, directing me after an apprenticeship at Halton, to a career as a navigator on Vulcans.

In this role I learned how to get from A to B, but still did not know where I was going. Whilst flying, though, I had the good fortune to visit America several times and there met Jack Stone, a warm-hearted Nebraskan who had founded the first franchise in a cleaning services business that had over 2000 outlets world-wide, my father owning one of them. So when Jack offered me a job I took it, resigned my commission, and prepared to move to the States.

I subsequently found myself out of the R.A.F. but without the relevant papers to get to the States. I later learned Jack had been on a turkey shoot for two months, which was why my papers were delayed. Meantime, I had to get a job, so I joined my father's business instead.

Why am I telling you all this? Well, my promotion within the U.K. chain of franchises that my father belonged to, led to my moving to Leicester and meeting Richard Denny, then with Leadership Development Limited. I duly attended one of their courses entitled "Success is a Science" and it was there that I learned, at the age of 29, about "taking charge of my own future." Everyone on the course but me was selling in the insurance industry, and, as often seemed to be the case, lied about their income! I was so excited by the possibilities of a financial services career that I decided to trade security and obscurity for riches, excitement and possible bankruptcy.

Now, seventeen years later, I've applied some of the rules from that first course plus a whole lot more learned along the way.
Through my speaking career I have mixed with some of the "great's" from my own industry and shared a lot of time with winners.
All of this has led to my building a unique library of information on how the personal growth formula actually works and how to set and achieve goals. This book is written to open up that library to you.

Nothing stays the same, if you've an extra idea for the library, write it on the pages at the back of the book where there's space to personalise this copy you have now acquired. The book itself is dedicated to all the people who have helped me along the way, and to Ann, my wife, who has given all my striving a reason and whose presence in my life has given me a true sense of purpose and personal fulfilment.

This book will............

Explain why goal setting works
Define the mental attitude you need to adopt to achieve your goals
Show you how to set personal goals.

Before you can set goals you must understand the way your mind works and adapt the way you think. Everything referred to here actually works. It has already been proven many times over and just needs you to apply it in your own life.

If you do, you will achieve everything you've ever wanted.

This book won't............

Achieve your goals for you
Contain everything ever said about goal setting
Replace the personal commitment needed to make your own goals a reality.

Distilled, to a few words, it says this:
Setting goals focuses your creative energy. You don't have to work ten times harder to achieve ten times as much. Dreams come true because you take **action.**

●   Use your potential

●   Change your future

●   Anything is possible

Contents

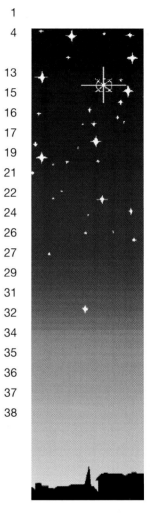

dream
big
dreams

Part Three - Mental Health 41

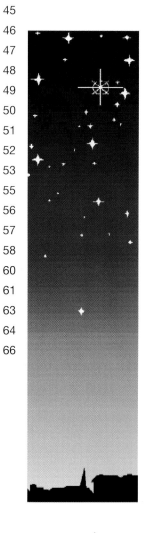

reach
for the
stars

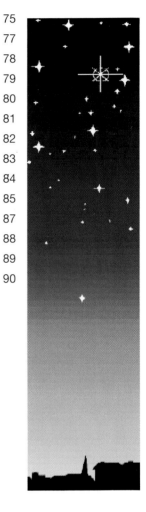

think
big

Part Six - Goals   93

there
are no
limits

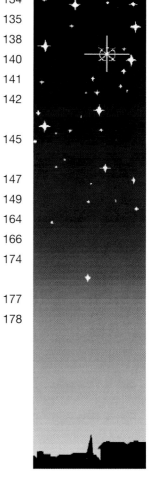

anything's
possible

Bibliography

I have found these books really valuable. They have assisted me in forming my views on personal goal setting.

Books

The Power of Positive Thinking	Norman Vincent Peale
Psycho-Cybernetics	Maxwell Maltz M.D.
Think and Grow Rich	Napoleon Hill
The Time Trap	R.A. Mackenzie
See You at the Top	Zig Ziglar
Time Power	Charles Hobbs
The Success System that Never Fails	W.C. Stone
Laws of Success	Napoleon Hill
Success Through a Positive Mental Attitude	Napoleon Hill & W.C.Stone
The Great Crossover	Dan Sullivan
The Seven Habits of Highly Effective People	Stephen Covey
Awaken the Giant Within	Anthony Robbins
Unlimited Power	Anthony Robbins
How I Raised Myself from Failure to Success in Selling	Frank Bettger
Maximum Achievement	Brian Tracy
The Road Less Travelled	Dr. Scott M. Peck

Audio programmes

"The Power of Goal Setting" by Paul J. Myers
Success Motivation Institute

"The Future is there for those who Invent it" by Louis Tice
Million Dollar Round Table Proceedings

"Goal Setting" by Zig Ziglar.

"The Psychology of Achievement" by Brian Tracy

Credits

I would like to thank the following people for assisting me in writing this book.

Firstly, Annie my wife for inspiring me and giving me the space to write it, my mother for always believing in me, Clive Holmes, founder of the Life Insurance Association of Great Britain, who gave me my first opportunity to speak on a main platform, the Life Insurance Congress at Wembley, England. Mervyn Scott my first manager at FPC Brokers who helped when things were difficult. Robin Fielder and Richard Denny for their Leadership Development Ltd course "Success is a Science" which set me off on the process of setting goals. Brian Tracy whose personal ideas on motivation are so thought provoking, Napoleon Hill for writing Think and Grow Rich, Zig Ziglar for being an inspiring and motivating speaker, Louis Tice for opening windows in my mind I did not know were there with his utterly thought provoking audio tape "The Future is there for those who Invent it". Paul J Myers for a classic tape on goal setting, "The Power of Goal Setting". Chris Myers for giving me my early tuition and encouragement on speaking. Frank Bettger for his common sense approach in "How I Raised Myself from Failure to Success in Selling". Dr Scott M. Peck who wrote the most moving book "The Road Less Travelled" a psychology on life and love. W. Clement Stone for "The Success System that Never Fails" and reminding me that inspirational dissatisfaction is the key motivator. The Life Insurance Association and all its' members for giving me the opportunity to develop my ideas whilst helping put something back into the industry that I passionately believe in. Million Dollar Round Table and Top of the Table, the most prestigious organisations in my own profession. Jack Hines from Montana aged 72 for reminding me that 72 can be the beginning of your life. Annie for typing the first version of this book, Lesley Wood for type setting the book at least three times, Paul Youle for co-ordinating the visuals and graphics and helping us all pull the book together on disc and of course all those who have heard me speak and wanted a copy of something more than just my notes which led to this book being created in the first place!

XV

part one

Can It Be True?

Note:

Throughout the book you'll see the intials

This is short for   **Must
Know**

You **must know** this part of the book it is a key fact that, if applied, will change your future.

Can it be True ?

Can you actually take charge of your own future? Can you make it do what you want it to do? Can you control events and trade mediocrity for your personal definition of success and achievement?

When I was told I could, I didn't believe it, and most people reading this book won't either.

It's not surprising, because most people never do 'trade up' to what they'd really like in life and consequently stay where they are.

Do people really want their heart's desire, and if they get it, will it make them happy?

Life's purpose, it seems to me, is to be the best you can be, and to achieve that in a way consistent with your personal values, so that having made progress, you can hang on to it because you believe you deserve it.

It's a bit like climbing a mountain. Before moving to the next hand or foot hold, you make sure the other three are firmly in place before moving upwards. Sometimes you only move by inches, but as you climb confidence in your ability grows, and the view changes, giving you a better perspective of where you are, where you've been and how to climb higher still.

Success is a journey, not a destination, and yes, you can have anything you want if deep down really want it.

What Exactly is Goal Setting?

Note: This chapter is designed to summarise the **essential** principles of goal setting in one chapter, parts of it are expanded in later chapters of the book.

Goal setting is a means of choosing and achieving everything you've ever wanted from life.

To understand why it works, we have to understand how our brain works.

Our brain is our personal computer, it is extraordinarily powerful and like any other computer it can be programmed.

Einstein believed that we only used 5% of our mental capacity. It is more likely that most of us consciously only use 1% to 2% of our true mental potential.

This leaves a vast reservoir of our computer capacity unused. This unused capacity can be consciously applied to achieve whatever we truly want from life.

So how does our computer work?

It's simple. There are two levels of consciousness in our brain.

the conscious
the subconscious

Our conscious mind reasons and decides, our subconscious mind **seeks to fulfil whatever our conscious mind decides**. The conscious mind itself is driven by our **opinions** or our circumstances. This means that our conscious opinions, not the **facts** themselves, form the basis of our conscious reasoning and in turn relay instructions to our subconscious for it to act upon. Our subconscious mind, on receiving our conscious mind's instructions, seeks to carry them out.

To repeat this fundamental point:

> our **conscious** mind reasons and decides
> our **subconscious** mind seeks to carry out the decisions that our conscious mind reaches.

So the subconscious mind is goal seeking by nature. It seeks to bring about whatever it has been asked to do by our conscious mind.

So **how has our subconscious been programmed so far?**

To understand this we need to be aware of Maslow's Theory of Hierarchical Needs.

Maslow states that there are five "drives" or "needs" in man. In sequence from the bottom up, they are:

> our "physiological" need
> our "security" need
> our "social" need
> our "esteem" need, and at the top of the pyramid
> our "self-fulfilment" need

Our lower order needs are born in us from birth and pursued intuitively without conscious thought or effort consequences. Our **physiological** need to breathe and eat are virtually automatic. Our **security** need, our instinct to be secure, and to avoid risk, is also, to a large extent, intuitive.

Ascending the scale from our **physiological** and **security** needs, our **social** and **esteem** needs are consciously pursued as we evaluate our potential in the world, in relation to our peer group.

The **"social"** drive to live in a particular locality and in a way consistent with our view of our position in life, and our drive for **"higher self-esteem"** means we also consciously work towards ensuring our **"social"** and **"esteem"** needs are fulfilled.

For most people, these four lower order drives, **physiological, security, social** and **esteem,** form the basis of our **entire life's efforts.**

Yet Maslow says **"self-fulfilment"** is our ultimate goal.

Most of us are not aware of this fact, cannot define self-fulfilment, don't know if we deserve it and don't know how to go about achieving it.

This book is written to answer the question "how do we achieve self-fulfilment?" and gives us a blue print to work from.

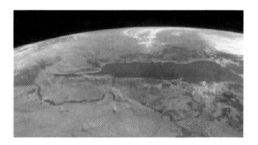

So far then, I repeat what I am saying......

Our subconscious mind works automatically and intuitively to ensure our **physiological** and **security** needs are met and with input from our conscious mind   sets about pursuing our **social** and **esteem** needs but rarely consciously pursues a higher order of **self-fulfilment.**

So we deny our brain, our computer, the one programme it needs to achieve our ultimate goal in life - **self-fulfilment,** because we do not know we can programme the brain to achieve that.

So there's good news and there's bad news.

The **good** news is that we **have** a computer that can be programmed to achieve all we desire.

The **bad** news is that we are not consciously programming it to accomplish our greatest aspiration, **self-fulfilment.**

Where's the proof?

The classic example quoted in **"Psycho Cybernetics"** by Dr. Maxwell Maltz is of a person who, on being hypnotised, is told to hold out the palm of his hand. He is then told that the hypnotist is going to place a red hot poker on his hand. The hypnotist then touches the subject's palm with the point of a pen, or pencil, and the person hypnotised **reacts as though it were a red hot poker**, to the extent, sometimes, that the skin will actually blister!

This demonstrates the enormous power of the subconscious and its' potential to react to and seek to fulfil any set of circumstances that it **believes** exists.

So where is this taking us?

1. The mind is a computer.

2. It can be programmed.

3. Our minds, with a few exceptions, have only been programmed to achieve the less fulfilling goals in life.

4. The subconscious seeks to bring about any set of circumstances, that it has been told exist by the conscious mind.

5. The conscious instructs the subconscious on the basis of its' opinion of the facts and **not** the facts themselves.

6. The subconscious mind cannot tell the difference.

7. If we programmed our mind, it would seek to ensure the outcome of the new programme just as easily as it carries out the old one.

What next?

Well, in computer language, we can assume GI = GO, Garbage In = Garbage Out, so if we give the brain nothing of significance to do, it just keeps on churning over the same matter.

So, what sort of programmes has our subconscious been programmed with so far?

Firstly all those pursued as per our lower order needs, as set out in Maslow's Theory, and **secondly**, those we have acquired along the way.

Where does this second set of programmes originate?

From our parents, family, friends, teachers and peers. Most of us are operating on programmes drummed into our subconscious by other people.

If you are 50 years of age, many of these programmes can be up to **40 years old.**

Question - Should we be driven **today** by 40 year old 'computer' programmes? **Wouldn't you rather free your own creativity, locked within you, to do the things you *really* want to do in life** that are relevant **now?**

You have the choice, and your computer will carry out whatever you choose, once you've decided what it is.

Where are we now?

1. Our mind is a computer.
2. It can be programmed.
3. With a few exceptions, it has usually only been programmed to achieve the less fulfilling goals in life.
4. Our subconscious mind seeks to bring about the circumstances it has been told exist by the conscious mind.
5. Our conscious mind instructs our subconscious mind on the basis of its' opinion of the facts and **not** on the facts themselves.
6. Our subconscious mind cannot tell the difference, and finally
7. We can re-programme our computer ourselves.

9

Yes, but does it work?

Will I have to work **five times harder** to achieve **five times as much?**

Am I going to have to be **twice as intelligent** if I want to accomplish **twice as much** in the future?

Will I be overwhelmed by the complexity of it all?

How do I get together all the things I need to achieve my goal?

Where will they come from?

How will I find them?........

All these questions are based on our logical belief of the way things get done. They are all based on the **wrong** assumption, which is, the assumption that success progresses in a logical way.

It doesn't!

1. You don't have to work five times harder, you just have to be better focused.

2. You don't have to be twice as smart, your desire to accomplish is far more important than your innate intelligence.

3. You don't get overwhelmed, because when you set your goals you filter out what you don't need

4. You don't have to assemble all the components for success and then get started, you set your **goal** and then you see, you do not see **then** set your goals.

And it works, so read on, absorb the philosophy of personal achievement handed on to us from the best thinkers and motivators of the last 100 years and see how your future will change.

The future is there for those who invent it, so start now, take charge and invent **your** future. After all destiny is not a matter of chance, it's a matter of choice.............!

part two

Human Potential

1.

Human Potential

"Capacity is a state of mind" Malcolm Kilminster

Surveys indicate that we use just a fraction of our potential. History demonstrates that man has the capacity to achieve virtually anything. To achieve more we have to develop a **"no limits"** belief in our potential. How? Read on.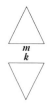

15

2.

Life

"Life is difficult. Once we truly know that life is difficult - once we understand and accept it - then life is no longer difficult". Dr. M. Scott Peck, M.D. - "The Road Less Travelled"

If it was easy everyone would have everything they ever wanted and there would be no pressure, stress or challenge.

Life isn't like that. Life asks us to be the best we can be, to pursue our goals and accomplish them and in doing so, achieve self-fulfilment.

We must give life our best shot.

3.

All Equal - all Entitled

"Ask, and it shall be given to you" St. Matthew Ch.7 v.7

We are all equal and all entitled, however, our past experiences, or "conditioning", limit what we **believe** we are entitled to.   This conditioning is imposed on society by the people who shape our beliefs and values from the moment we are born.   In creating order for the majority of society we are encouraged and taught to **comply** and **conform**. The "fabric" of society, evolved by those who went before us and upheld by those who'd like to see the *status quo* maintained, encourages us to **conform** and not "buck" the system.

This application of the lowest common denominator limits most of us, keeping us "in our place" where **sadly** most of us remain.

Most of us therefore never reach for the stars because we are too conditioned by society's "rules" to ever consider breaking them.

Paul J Myers, on his great tape "The Power of Goal Setting" said "You can go to God with a cup or a bucket. Most people go with a sieve, they expect nothing so they get nothing". So we are conditioned to accept our lot and not encouraged to question the order of things. It doesn't matter whether we are born into a poor family or a wealthy one, we become conditioned to our circumstances and generally accept them without question.

Capacity

"Man cannot pass beyond the bounds of self-imposed limitation". Anon.

An elephant born in captivity, tethered by a metal chain during its infancy, becomes aware of the chain's strength and realises it cannot break it. As it grows the chain will be swapped for a rope but the elephant on feeling the rope tugging on its ankle doesn't try and break the rope because it **thinks it can't.**

A barracuda put into a fish tank with a mackerel will eat the mackerel. If you divide the tank with a sheet of glass, put the barracuda one side and the mackerel the other, the barracuda sees the mackerel and will swim towards it to try to eat it. The glass stops it and after a while finding it can't break the glass the barracuda stops trying.

If you take the glass out, the barracuda doesn't try to eat the fish because it **thinks it can't.**

It happened to me too when I took up running. I decided to start jogging to lose weight. I had run **two** to **three** miles in cross-country at school so I knew I could run that far. I began running **two** to **three** miles a day again, then one day I got lost and ran **seven** miles by accident!

I knew I could run two miles but didn't believe I could run **seven**. Once I realised I could run **seven** miles by accident, I decided to run **ten** miles by design, and did! Then **thirteen**. Then **twenty-six**. **Twenty-six** miles is over **ten** times further than the two miles I knew I could run.

So I have a question for you. Who set the limit on my potential? **I did. We all do.**

To overcome these limiting beliefs, we have to develop a "no limits" belief in our potential. We are capable of achieving anything we deep-down truly want to achieve, and **only we set the limits on what is possible.**

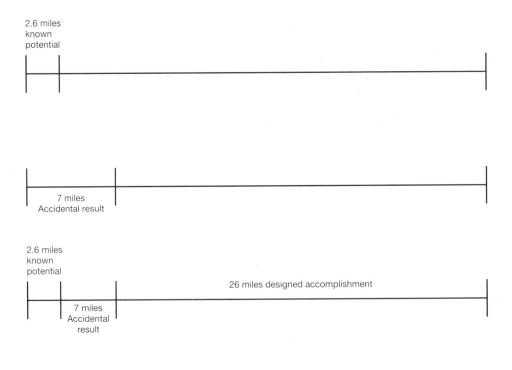

2.6 miles
known
potential

7 miles
Accidental result

2.6 miles
known
potential

26 miles designed accomplishment

7 miles
Accidental
result

5.

Unlimited Capacity.

"Anything's possible". Anon

We all have the capacity to achieve whatever we **deep-down truly desire and will commit ourselves to achieving.**

6.

Our Flight Envelope

"If you think you can, you can, if you think you can't you can't, whether you think you can or you can't - you're right" Henry Ford.

Once we've learned from our environment and internalised 'the rules', we operate **within** them and it usually takes an extraordinary event to take us beyond them. When studying aerodynamics, the science of flight, I was taught that an aircraft wing will lift the aircraft as long as its angle of attack is set within certain pre-determined limits. If the wing's angle is outside these parameters, lift is lost, and the aircraft falls out of the sky.

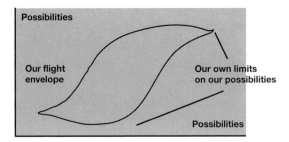

The graphic representation of this is known as "the flight envelope".

We all have our own flight envelope. Its shape is determined by the limits we set for ourselves. Unless told or shown otherwise, we continue to operate within those limits, never venturing outside them, in case, just like the aircraft, we fall out of the sky.

But our flight envelope, our limitations, are mainly set **for** us by other people who have decided for us, what's "possible".

These people are not us. They cannot know what we might achieve.

7.

The Comfort Zone

"Every man is a self-made man, only the successful ones admit it".

Our flight envelope is our "comfort zone".

We feel secure if we stay within it and because most people feel the same way, it seems perfectly normal to comply with the "rules" we set ourselves.

As a result most people settle for a life of frustration and quiet desperation, never daring to be more than they already are.

We are as great as our most dominant aspiration and as small as our greatest fear.

We all operate between two limits, an upper and a lower, based on our expectations of ourselves. The upper limit is as high as our most dominant aspiration, the lower limit as low as our greatest overriding fear.

Each day we operate between the aspiring levels we are comfortable with, and are afraid of descending to the lowest. When we get on a "roll" we operate at the upper limit of our opinion of our right to success. When we get a "down" we fall as far as we feel we can respectably fall without letting ourselves down. These two limits are the outer edges of our comfort zone. We feel "safe" within these two limits and take just enough action to keep us firmly fixed somewhere in the middle.

Our fear of exceeding our expectations, or of failing, steals our potential. It renders our greatest dreams stillborn. Fear forces us to accept whatever we feel society allows rather than what we'd really like.

To excel, we have to get out of our comfort zone, break out of our flight envelope and release the potential for greatness locked inside of us.

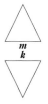

8.

Using Our Potential to Achieve - the Choice is Ours

"Man is designed for accomplishment, engineered for success and endowed with the seeds of greatness". Zig Ziglar

Our potential is there within us, whether we use it or not, it is there. The seeds of greatness are within us all, freely given and ours to use if we care to. **Only we can decide whether we will.**

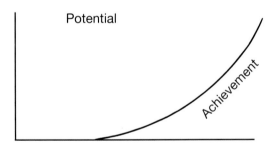

9.

Most People

"Dare mighty things even though checkered with failure, rather than rank with those grey souls that know neither victory nor defeat".
Theodore Roosevelt.

So most people are happy within their comfort zone. No risk, no challenge, nothing gained, nothing lost. Do we have to be most people? Are we destined to be? What are **most people** like?

Imagine this. If you were offered £1,000,000 today, with no obligation except to spend it, you'd probably accept it. Yes?

But what if you had to give up something for it? Something really valuable. What about your right arm? Would you do it? Would you give up your right arm for £1,000,000 ?

Most of us would not. So here we are with one arm worth at least £1,000,000. Let's take stock and check our inventory. That means we have £2,000,000 for our two arms, probably another £2,000,000 for our two legs and at least £2,000,000 for our two eyes. So the minimum we'd price ourselves at is £6,000,000!

Question: If we are worth at least **£6,000,000** how come most of us rent our brains out for less than **£30,000** a year? Why? **Because most people do.**

But we are not most people.

We are individuals. We are **unique** with an **unlimited capacity** to achieve, and to use the massive reserves of our largely untapped mental potential.

So we don't have to settle for £30,000 a year, we can choose to do otherwise. We simply do not have to do what other people do.

10.

Human Needs - Maslow's Theory

*"We're all born under the same sky
but we don't all have the same horizon"*
Konrad Adenauer

Self Fulfilment
Esteem
Social
Security
Physiological

Maslow's Theory of Hierarchical Needs

Maslow's Theory of Hierarchical Needs states that human beings strive to fulfil five needs.

In ascending order starting with man's primary physiological needs, these are:

1.   **The Physiological need**
        The need to breathe, eat, and to drink to sustain life.

2.   The Security need
The need to be secure, live in a safe environment where we lead a normal life without threat.

3.   The Social need
Living in a locality that reflects our belief of our status, with social activities that reflect this vision of our "status".

4.   The Esteem need
The need to be recognised within our social group. This need drives us to acquire things and do things that confirm to ourselves that we are "doing well".

5.   The Fifth need
Most people are not consciously aware of this one, yet it is the most important of all the needs in terms of reward and gratification.

It is the need **for self-fulfilment.**

The most significant drive in our life is the **need to fulfil ourselves**, to know we've strived to use our full potential, and although self-fulfilment enriches us more than any other need, it is neither discussed or consciously pursued by most people.

11.

Motivation

"The world makes way for a man who knows wherever he is going"
Ralph Waldo Emerson

Everyone is motivated. Some are motivated to achieve, others are motivated to stay as they are, but all of us are motivated.

To achieve a goal, a person has to be motivated to achieve that specific goal. We will only leave our "comfort zone" if we are sufficiently motivated to do so. Setting personal goals of real meaning creates the stimulus to leave our "comfort zone".

12.

Self-Image

"Really successful people all seem to have one thing in common: they expect more good out of life than bad. They expect to succeed more often than they expect to fail." Henry F. McCamish, Jr., CLU

Maxwell Maltz explains in "Psycho-cybernetics" that we perform in a manner consistent with how we see ourselves, our self-image. The **facts** do not count. It is our opinions that determine the way in which we perform.

Here's an example:

The local professional coach at the golf club learns that an international tournament is to take place at his club and knowing the course, naturally he enters. In the first round, highly motivated, he plays the round of his life against the world's greatest golfers. His first round is a 65.

The headlines read **"Local pro leads the field!"**

On the second day he goes out again. This time he goes round in 66. He's now tied for the lead with the world's leading money maker in golf that year. He's delighted, but also intimidated to be measured alongside the world's greatest golfers. The second day's headlines read: **"Local hero tied for the lead."**

Now he is playing like he's never played before and can't believe he's tied for the lead. Is he really that good? Surely not?

The third day comes. He goes round in 86 and is relegated to thirteenth place. Next day the headlines read: **"Local challenge fades"**. Now what does he think to himself? How's he feeling? What's running through his mind? "This is where I expected to be. These are the world's greatest, after all. I did well for two rounds, but I didn't really expect I would win."

So how's he feeling? Sad? Disappointed? Not a bit of it! **He's happy**. Why? Because his performance is consistent with his expectation of himself.

He had a hard time dealing with seeing himself on top. Seeing himself as beating the world's number one was just too much to believe, so he **sabotaged** his own success rather than win and expose himself to the need to adjust his perception of himself, his status and his future.

He was out of his comfort zone and took action, unconsciously, to ensure that he stayed within it. We all perform in a manner consistent with our image of ourselves.

To change this self-image, we have to change our opinion of ourselves. This can only be done by taking the necessary **actions** to adjust our self-belief. Our opinion of ourself must change.

13.

Past Events

"We cannot direct the wind but we can adjust the sails".

The pain or the pleasure of a past event is remembered when the same situation arises again, and the pain, or the pleasure associated with that event comes to mind and is remembered.

We go into the new situation carrying the memory of our emotional reaction to that situation last time it occurred.

The emotional imprint we carry from our past will colour our belief as to our chances of success or failure whenever we meet the same situation again.

To succeed permanently, we need a healthy self-image and a good opinion of ourselves.

Getting thrown by a horse can lead either to a fear of riding for life, or, the opportunity to conquer the fear if you get back on the horse immediately and try again.

14.

Opinions

"Its all in the mind"

Our opinions are more powerful than the facts.

Here's an example.

If you were walking through a forest and a large bear jumped out in front of you, you'd probably run as fast as possible to get away from the bear. It wouldn't matter at that moment if it was a man dressed up as a bear or a real bear. Your opinion of what you see and the danger you believe it creates **is more important** than the facts themselves.

You wouldn't stop to check it out you'd just get away from the bear as fast as possible, whether it was a bear **or** a man dressed as one.

You behave in the manner consistent with your belief of the event, not the facts themselves. Which is the most important, the facts or our **opinion?**

15.

Success Experiences

*"I would rather attempt something great and fail,
than to attempt nothing and succeed"*
James A Van Houten

Success experiences. We need to fill our memory with **success** experiences and **positive** events that we can call upon to displace previous, more dominant "negative" events.

Setting and achieving goals in all areas of our life gives us the opportunity to build up these success experiences. The simplest goal achieved is one more positive event re-affirming our personal worth. The more we displace any history of past negative events with positive achievements the more we will habitually **expect** to win.

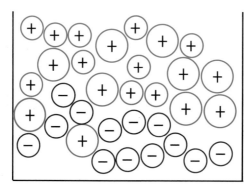

Our successful experiences are stored and as they add up
they gradually displace our negative experiences

16.

Personal Growth

"To grow, you must get out of your comfort zone".
Robert J Wernecke

Maslow's theory of hierarchical needs says that self-fulfilment represents the pinnacle of our achievement in life.

It is the desire to be better, **and be the best we can be** in the time we are given.

Whatever we do in life that demands of us, tests us. We are being asked to extend ourselves, to enlarge our capacity to achieve, and to develop greater qualities and strengths within ourselves.

We are given life to experience personal growth, and through that experience to achieve our maximum potential.

Our purpose in life is to use our potential to its fullest. To pursue excellence We are on earth to be the best we can be. Any shirking of that steals from ourselves. By setting higher goals for ourselves and by aspiring to greatness, whether we win or lose we fulfil ourselves through the knowledge that we did everything we could to be the best.

17.

Winners

"Winners expect to win in advance. Life is a self-fulfilling prophecy".

If we use our full potential, we will be seen by others to be a winner. What single characteristic distinguishes a winner from a loser?

Winners have belief without evidence. The mediocre look for the evidence before they believe.

Winners having decided what they want, have faith that the conditions they need to win **will** occur, or that they will "make their own luck" and change the conditions they need to ensure that they win.

Mediocre people either have no faith, or are lacking confidence in their own ability and look for the evidence that confirms they'll succeed before acting.

part two
summary

Lessons learned

_____
_____
_____
_____
_____

Questions to ask

_____
_____
_____
_____
_____

Actions to take

_____
_____
_____
_____
_____

39

part three

Mental Health

18.

Opening Remarks

*"We cannot attract and keep anything that we do not truly believe
we are entitled to "*

Understanding how our mind works will help us to perform successfully, consistently, and to be at peace with ourselves. We can only achieve this by deciding what beliefs we do hold to be true, and then living in a way that is consistent with those beliefs.

Our mental health will be good if we are true to our beliefs. The lack of stress that stems from this forms the foundation from which balanced and honest actions arise. These enacted in our daily lives, **will make the permanent attainment** of our goals more likely, and because we are acting in a manner consistent with our beliefs, much less stressful.

19.

Self-Esteem

"Happiness is not a state to arrive at, but rather a manner of travelling"
Samuel Johnson

"I can't love you if I don't love myself". To love other people, we have first to love ourselves.

A healthy self-esteem is created by acting in a way that is consistent with your underlying beliefs of good and bad.

Living by the standards we set ourselves, creates a positive image of our own lives.

What we then achieve we are entitled to keep, and deep down truly deserve.

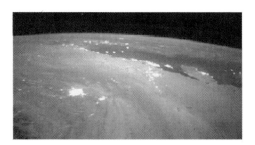

20.

Stress and Distress

"Stress is what happens when you set a goal and a deadline for its' accomplishment, - it's a positive asset when energised in the pursuit of that goal" Malcolm Kilminster

Striving for goals that are inconsistent with our personal principles always leads to **distress**. This damages our mental heath. It impairs our ability to function properly. To stop this happening we need to understand the difference between **distress** and **stress**.

Distress is harmful to us. Things initially beyond our control will impose a pressure upon us and we can do little about the distress this causes if the source of conflict is not within our direct control. **A certain amount of stress however, is not harmful**. A little stress improves our performance. Too much stress however, and we may buckle under the pressure.

Setting a goal, having a target to attain by a specific deadline, is a deliberate means of imposing stress on ourselves. This self-imposed stress acts as a stimulant and calls on us to use our creativity and ingenuity to achieve our goal.

$$\frac{\bigtriangleup}{m}$$
$$\frac{k}{\bigtriangledown}$$

To live with distress is to be out of control.   x

To create stress to stimulate the achievement √
of a goal, is to be in control.

45

21.

Love

"Freely ye received, freely give" St. Matthew ch.10 v 8

It is very difficult for any goal that has a direct effect on other people to be pursued, honestly attained, and held onto unless you have an intrinsic love of other people.

Most goals require the co-operation of others and are only achieved through an exchange of real value one person to another. For real value to be exchanged, the goal itself must be based on the principle of **win, win**. For our achievements to have long-term value, they must involve a genuine desire on our part to care about the outcome and that, in turn, has at its heart a love of other people.

Love is pure, clean and certain. It is also unequivocal and asks nothing in return. It should not be given in the belief that it will be reciprocated because that anticipates another person's actions and seeks to control the other person's reactions. How the other person reacts is for them to decide and we should not seek control. We must love unconditionally.

22.

Cynicism

"I don't believe in pessimism. If something doesn't come up the way you want, forge ahead. If you think its going to rain, it will"
Clint Eastwood

Cynics expect the worst. They are pessimistic about any outcome. To be cynical is to deny that human life has any meaning or value. You can't care deeply for the future of the human race, or pursue personal growth, or help others, if you are cynical.

There is no "middle ground". Either you care deeply and passionately in the potential of people, even if you are seen as naive for doing so, or you discard life as meaningless.

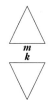

A cynic cannot achieve worthwhile goals. Cynics should be avoided at all costs. They destroy your drive and creativity.

23.

Optimism

"People rarely exceed their dreams"
Millard J Grauer

Optimism is the expression of faith in the future outcome of events.

Optimism is an essential part of the goal setting process. Expecting the best is part of achieving any goal.

Failing

"In great attempts it is glorious to fail"
Cassius

Failure is never final. Failure is temporary. Learn from failure and then put it aside. Focus on the future success you expect to accomplish. Press on towards your goal. A failure experience shows you one way that the objective you had in mind couldn't be accomplished, that's all.

Thomas Eddison was asked by a reporter why he had failed to invent the light bulb filament 9,000 times. He replied "I have not failed 9,000 times, I've found 9,000 ways it doesn't work".

Failure triumphs if we quit , but only if we quit. If we persist, it cannot defeat us.

25.

Fear of Failure

"Our doubts are traitors and make us lose the good we oft might win by fearing to attempt" William Shakespeare

To fear failure is illogical. If we've failed at something in the past the next time we attempt to achieve our goal, **everything** relating to our previous failure will have changed. We are different, the circumstances are different and the obstacles are different. The probability of failing will be entirely different. It is illogical to be afraid that a past failure will repeat itself.

The only way to overcome failure is to persist, press on.

26.

Why do we Fear Failure?

"Pity the man who fears failure and never makes a beginning"
Patrick W Corcoran

Fear damages our **opinion** of ourselves. It diminishes our self-esteem and lowers our **opinion** of our self-worth.

To use life positively we should see failure and success simply as information. Failure and success experiences give us information and that information helps us take the next action needed in the pursuit of success. **Neither** experience is damaging. Both teach us something.

Used positively, failure is as much an asset as success.

27.

Opinion and its Effect on You

"The act of believing creates strength."

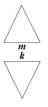

Our opinions of ourselves are stronger than the facts.
We behave in accordance with our belief in our opinions.

This means that our opinions are **more important** than the facts. As we spend 98% of our time talking to ourselves we must be careful that we do not form permanent negative views about ourselves.

Our opinions determine our "Self-Image" and a strong positive self-image only comes about if we decide to believe in ourselves. We must therefore work on believing in our qualities and set out to strengthen them. The "spiritual" area of our goal setting gives us the opportunity to add value to ourselves. We should take those areas where we feel weak and reverse them with positive goals and positive affirmations:

    Goal: To be more confident
    Affirmation: I am more confident

This stream of positive thoughts will improve your self-image and your sense of personal worth. It will make you stronger.

52

28.

Change

"Most men live lives of quiet desperation"

We are the sum total of everything we have ever thought about, and to that extent are at ease with who we are now. Most of us are relatively relaxed about the person we are now and at least we believe we know who we are.

A change in ourselves presents us with the prospect of becoming someone else, someone we don't know, someone with whom we are not familiar. This new person is unknown to us and cannot be clearly seen. As we instinctively avoid the unknown, anything we cannot see clearly makes us wary.

The reluctance to change is often so great that you can probably think now of people, we know from our own life experiences, who are so conditioned by society and habits that they make a virtue out of never changing. These people can often be intimidating, but it is worth remembering that with closed minds they live their lives in a mummified condition, "dying" at thirty and ending up being buried at eighty.

These people are easy to recognise. Their motto is "My mind's made up, don't confuse me with the facts." They feel safe through not changing.

Fear of change can be transformed, we can control it and transform it into optimism if we decide **who** it is we'd like to be, instead of letting society, our friends, complete strangers, conditions, environment, and our own lack of vision decide for us.

By choosing who we are, we dispel fear. To be freed up in this way is such an amazing feeling. All the historic "I can't because....." excuses, vanish if we embrace change positively.

29.

Afraid to Try

"Expect to accomplish what you attempt"

We always over-estimate the opposition, and always under-estimate our capacity to overcome the odds. This mental magnification, exaggerated by the consequence of failing dominates our power of visualisation. We magnify the obstacles.

$$\frac{m}{k}$$

It's **fear** again. The fear of trying. What might we lose if we try? The fear exists because we cannot see the future.

Our uncertainty about the future is dispelled if we decide what our future will contain and set our own goals for ourselves so that **we** control that future.

Goal setting gives us the freedom to choose what our future contains and dispels the fear of trying.

30.

Timing - When is it the Right Time?

"Fear vanishes when imagination ceases and action begins"
Arlen I. Prentice

Will I do better if I wait until:

- The economy improves?
- I know more?
- I've got better prospects?
- I get better equipment?
- My boss is in a better mood?
- I've saved more money?
- Interest rates are lower?

There is never a right time. Putting off the decision to try is to take a rest, to procrastinate. There will never be a right time. The only way to overcome the problem of procrastination is to **act**. Take action now. There'll never be a better time.

The good old days are here and now.

31.

Talking to Ourselves

"The pessimist sees difficulty in every opportunity. The optimist sees opportunity in every difficulty". Winston Churchill

We spend 98% of our lives in conversation with ourselves. We don't talk out loud, usually, but we talk nonetheless. What do we say to ourselves? Is it good or bad? Does it contain the seeds of self-doubt, or optimism?

We owe it to ourselves to speak positively about ourselves.

32.

How to Change Positively

"If it is to be, it is up to me"

To change ourselves, we must take stock of who we are **now** and then plan the changes in ourselves.

1.   List your strengths and weakness
2.   Prioritise the weakness, put the one troubling you most first, the least troubling last.
3.   Select the weakness you'd like to change the most.
4.   Re-state the weakness in writing as a **positive goal**.
5.   Write down the **affirmation** to go with the positive goal.
6.   Start a 30-day repetitive plan of reading the positive goal and affirmation.

The only way to break an old habit is to create a new one. To do this, you must habitually repeat the same set of actions daily. A period of 30 days will set the new habit in place and the weakness will be reversed. Delete the weakness from your weakness list and add the reciprocal new strength by your list of strengths. Here's an example:

Strengths		Weaknesses	
I'm optimistic	√	I am a poor time keeper	x
I'm confident	√	I am a poor listener	x
I'm a good listener	√	I lack concentration	x
I'm cheerful	√	I get depressed	x

Worst weakness

"I'm a poor timekeeper."

Re-state as a goal

"I will be on time for every appointment I make."

Re-state as a positive affirmation

"I am always on time for appointments."

Read both the positive goal and the positive affirmation at least six times daily for 30 days. This will form a new habit that you can follow for good.

Select the next weakness

"I am a poor listener"

Re-state as a positive goal

"I will listen carefully to the person I am speaking with."

Re-state as a positive affirmation

"I am a good listener."

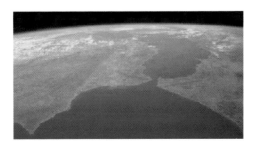

33.

We Become What we Think About

"Your living is determined not so much by what life brings you, as by what happens to you, as by the way your mind looks at what happens"
John H Miller

The principle of affirmation, of "assuming a virtue we don't have", demonstrates that if we implant an idea in our subconscious minds by sending positive messages via the conscious mind we can change.

If we want to be more enthusiastic, for example, we say:
> **"I am enthusiastic"**
> **"I am enthusiastic"**
> **"I am enthusiastic"**

and the subconscious creates the conditions for it to be so.
We will become what we think about.

If we don't pass positive affirmation messages to the subconscious everything carries on just as before with positive and negative messages being passed at random.

It is obvious then that we must keep feeding positive **"yes I can"** messages into our subconscious and avoid passing negative messages.

34.

Perspective

"You must have long-term goals to avoid being defeated by short-term failure"

You get up in the morning, get ready for work, and start your journey to work by car. You get to the first set of traffic lights. They are red. You turn round, go home, get undressed and go back to bed. **True or false? - False!**

So why do people driving on life's journey on seeing an obstacle, turn round and give up? The answer? No perspective.

Without a clear plan for the future, today's obstacle can be seen as permanent. With no clear long-term objective in sight today's problem blocks us from proceeding.

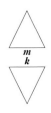

The answer is to get a grip on life's long-term perspective. Here's how.

Breaking through.

Take a six inch ruler. Draw a horizontal line and mark off the 60 tenths of an inch. Each tenth of an inch is a year of your own life. So each tenth is 365 days long. Now mark off the 3 or 4 days within that one tenth of an inch that represents the 3 or 4 days you feel depressed. How long is the line, can you see it? It's too small to see isn't it?

INCHES

Yet people give up after just 3 or 4 days depression, they think the world is coming to an end. Its just not true, but it seems that way at the time if we've no long-term perspective.

With a five year plan, a four day obstacle is not an insurmountable problem. It's not an irreversible event, it's only an obstacle to overcome.

35.

Waiting for Permission to Perform

"There is never a right time" Anon.

Most people wait for permission before going ahead and growing.

They stop, caught at an imaginary red traffic light, waiting for someone else to change the lights to green before they go forward.

There's a difference between resting or pausing for a moment, and sitting around until someone says "yes, you can". **You can now.**

Don't procrastinate. If you want it, get on and start working for it **NOW.**

36.

Peer Group Pressure - The Desire to Conform

*"Two men look out through the same bars; one sees mud,
the other sees stars"* Frederick Langbridge

Peer group pressure will be found where any group is gathered. It might be your family, your relations, your fellow pupils, your colleagues at work, your immediate social circle, or your team mates if you play sports.

In each of these groups, it is so much easier to fall in line to get along with other members of the group.

It's a part of most peoples' nature to want to be liked, to be polite and it's always going to be easier to experience those feelings if you get along with the majority.

But they are not you, and what's more, most of them are not usually bothered about you one way or the other. They do however, like most human beings, enjoy an audience and you are part of that audience. Most of them are too busy working on their own lives to be intensely involved with your personal struggle for success. **Do what's best for you**. Don't hurt others, but **be true to your own needs**. Time lost in drifting with the crowd can never be won back and rarely helps you in the long run.

It'll make you feel good now, but it steals your most valuable asset, time, and the use of your most valuable talent, your intellect, to plan and achieve your own future.

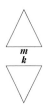

37.

Balance and the Absence of Guilt

"A person will be just about as happy as they make up their minds to be"
Abraham Lincoln

Balance is knowing when you **are** goal achieving, and have a clear plan of how to accomplish your goals, knowing when you are **not** goal achieving, and are entitled to tension relieving time.

We should be clear with ourselves as to when we should and should not be working. Distress is caused from the imbalances in our lives. We should agree with ourselves on when we intend to be goal achieving and positive stress is present, and when we will be tension relieving and there will be no work related stress.

The amount of time we spend tension relieving is not important. It's the quality of the time that we reward ourselves with when we've stopped goal achieving that counts. We can look forward to just one hour in a day or just one day in the month when we do something for ourselves away from goal achieving. We don't need huge amounts of rest or tension relieving time. We only need a lot of tension relieving time when we are out of step with the goal achieving part of our lives.

part three
summary

Lessons learned

_____

_____

_____

_____

_____

Questions to ask

_____

_____

_____

_____

_____

Actions to take

_____

_____

_____

_____

_____

part four

Physical Health

70

38.

Health

"To help others we must first help ourselves"
Malcolm Kilminster

We are not able to focus on achieving meaningful goals if we are impaired through ill health.

We can't avoid hereditary ill health, but we can create the right conditions for good health.

These will all damage our ability to concentrate or see clearly what we wish to accomplish:
- alcohol
- drugs
- cigarettes
- obesity
- unbalanced diet
- excessive caffeine
- lack of exercise

We can act to avoid these excesses and situations. We should do so. It is difficult to focus energy on goal achieving if a large part of our energy is dissipated by overcoming self-inflicted impediments.

39.

Physical Condition

"The body is the temple of the soul" Anon.

Dr. Kenneth Cooper the man who devised aerobics, has over 30,000 clients who subscribe to his health clinics in Dallas, Texas. He says that the level of physical activity needed to be healthy is remarkably low.

If we take four weekly exercise periods of at least twenty minutes, we can remain in relatively good physical condition.

The ideal level of aerobic exercise should leave you slightly puffing when you finish the exercise. Cardiovascular exercise i.e. the heart in steady, rhythmic activity such as running, swimming, jogging, cycling or brisk walking is one of the most beneficial things we can do to improve our life expectancy.

Increasing the circulation of blood through the additional intake of oxygen created through exercise is intoxicating. The natural release of endorphins whilst exercising creates a natural "high" and a feeling of well-being.

Exercise is good for you - do it!

40.

Diet

"You are what you eat" Anon.

Rapid weight loss diets are not usually of help in the long run as often the weight goes back on again sometime later when you are less watchful. You can remove excess fat from your body by removing fat from your diet. In this way your body burns your own fat because there is no new fat intake.

At the time of writing, there are continuing arguments as to the benefits of polyunsaturated and unsaturated fats and the best advice is just to reduce the amount of fat you eat. To avoid the tiredness, that usually occurs after eating it's also worth considering the Hay Diet. This is based on not mixing carbohydrates with proteins and starches in the same meal. This avoids the internal conflict in your digestive system that creates drowsiness.

Eating fruit gives you energy. It releases natural sugars and improves your mental sharpness. I only eat fruit until 12 each day. By snacking on fruit when I'm hungry, I'm able to obtain the natural sugar in fruit to give me energy. Avoiding bread and other fattening foods for at least half of each day has had a direct impact on my weight and my mental alertness and by not mixing carbohydrates and proteins in the same meal, I find I'm mentally sharper. Try it. It could help you too.

part four
summary

Insights gained

_____

_____

_____

_____

_____

Questions to ask

_____

_____

_____

_____

_____

Actions to take

_____

_____

_____

_____

_____

part five

Success

41.

Success

"To succeed is to live, everything else is to wait" Anon.

A faint hope, or a predictable event?

Success can be achieved by applying basic principles. These basic principles are as predictable as gravity, and can be applied by anyone.

There's nothing mysterious about achievement. All of us are born equal. It's our conditioning and environment that affect how we do in life. When a baby is born, lying in the maternity ward it has a wrist tag. It shows the baby's name. It doesn't say "dustman, doctor, teacher or labourer". As we grow up our beliefs are formed by our experiences, our parents' circumstances and their attitudes, and the attitude of our teachers. They all teach us what they can, alongside the passive teachers of the media, television and radio. They all affect our possibilities, and chances of success.

At that point we neither choose or control our environment and to be successful, we must find a success environment. We immerse ourselves in it thinking and acting as successful people.

77

42.

Success Conditioning and Self-Image

"Mind is everything, we become what we think" Guatama Buddha

Our mind is like a tape recorder. It remembers **everything** we have ever done and our emotional response. Success or failure at an activity in our past affects how we feel about that activity now. To succeed now we need to dismiss negative emotions from the past and create an environment where success occurs as often as possible.

Experiencing continual successes, no matter how small, continually reinforces the emotions associated with succeeding and being successful.

No matter how small the victories, they strengthen your self-image and self-worth. See how the way you work can be adapted to create success experiences, victories for doing well. Look for "personal bests" bench marks of excellence based on your highest results in a day, a week, a month, a year. Make winning a game. Play to win and strengthen your self-esteem while doing so. It's fun and it makes you stronger.

Success conditioning occurs when the person involved is continually having their memory reinforced and their mind conditioned with the feelings experienced from succeeding and being successful. This leads to an "I don't know how to fail" attitude and massively improves the self-image of the person experiencing these feelings.

43.

Desire

"Its our desire not our ability that determines our success".

Nothing of value is achieved that is not first fuelled by desire. Desire can be positive , or negative.
Whichever it is, it is the ingredient that compels you to take action.

Positive desires   - to do better
                                  - to be the best
                                  - to set a new record
                                  - to be recognised

Negative desires   - to avoid taking a risk
                                  - to get something for as little as possible

Desire is the stimulus, and without it nothing happens. How do you create desire ?

By deciding what you really want from life. Which in turn creates **inspirational dissatisfaction** with your present situation.

The desire to improve is the key to setting goals.

44.

Being in Charge of Your Own Future

"Take action"
W. Clement Stone

We cannot achieve the things we set our heart on if our position in life is wrong.

For example, we will not earn unlimited sums of money if we accept a salaried position working for someone else, and just wish and hope for a better future. We have to switch from being paid by the hour to being paid by results.

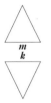

If you can't control your future, move jobs now.
You can't invent your own future if you are working for an inventor.
You must become the inventor yourself.

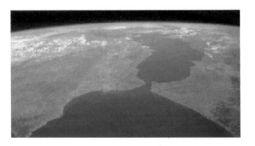

45.

Academic Ability

"Once you say you're going to settle for second that's what happens to you in life"
John F Kennedy

Your academic results have no bearing on how much you will achieve in your life. Ralph Waldo Emerson wrote that a stock clerk in a factory with a burning desire to succeed could be made into a winner, but a university graduate with no desire to succeed could soon be put to work as a stock clerk in a factory. He meant that desire is more important than ability. It's true.

Our desire is more important than our ability.

A deep down desire to succeed is our principle motivator.

In what direction will our motivation take us? That depends on the destination **we** set, and that is determined by the objectives we set for ourselves.

46.

Attitude

"It's our attitude not our aptitude that determines our altitude".

If we think we can, we can, if we think we can't, we can't, whether we think we can or think we can't we're probably right.

How we see a situation largely determines the outcome. If we believe we can solve a situation this immeasurably contributes towards our ability to solve it.

Our attitude, not our aptitude determines our altitude.

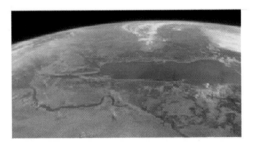

47.

The Positive Use of Motivation

"It concerns us to know the purpose we seek in life, for then, like archers aiming at a definitive mark, we shall be more likely to attain what we want" Aristotle.

Our goals give our motivation a specific direction.

Without goals we are aimless. That doesn't mean that we won't be happy. Lots of people are very happy wanting nothing and going nowhere. We have already seen that they're in their comfort zone, and will be able, as in Newton's Laws of Physics, to remain in a state of rest unless acted upon by an external force.

Goals are the objectives that create the desire, and motivation is that desire in motion towards the objectives we have selected.

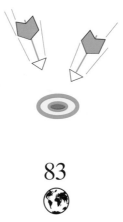

48.

Positive Thinking

"If you think you can, you can"
Henry Ford.

If we become what we think about, hadn't we better decide what sort of person we want to be?

There are just two attitudes we can adopt. It's clearly black and white there is no grey. We are either:

Positive thinkers
or
Negative thinkers

We are either positively building our self-image in our minds, or destroying our self-esteem through being negative.

Positive thinking asks that we see things in a certain way. We expect the best and we look for the good. Positive thinking builds our strength of conviction, it makes us stronger and helps us achieve more.

Negative thinking is destructive. It steals our potential to succeed. Avoid negative people.

49.

Positive Thinking Habits

"The positive thinker creates a majority".

1. Looking for the good in a situation

If you don't, you accept what you are "under the circumstances" and accept that you cannot control the outcome of a situation. This is an abdication of our responsibility to ourselves.

We must say "there is some good in this situation," so that we can profit from that experience.

We cannot always control whether a good thing or a bad thing will happen to us but we can control how we react, or control how we feel about the situation.

We should always say "How can I get the best out of this situation?"

2. See what can be, not what is

Look forward from now on and see where you are going. Be optimistic and expect good things to come about. That will then help them to happen.

3. Add value

Practice complimenting, thanking and praising people. People like recognition and their performance improves if you encourage them.

4. Be a "How Can I Do it Better?" person

Always seek to improve the way things are done. **Pursue excellence in whatever you do.**

5. Avoid words that imply a limitation to your potential

Avoid phrases such as "I'll try", and "I can't". These imply limitation.

6. Use positive language

Don't allow negative words into your conversations, avoid the use of words such as problem, substitute situation. We can sort out situations, we find it harder to solve problems. The word creates an emotive response in those tackling it.

7. Act as though success was inevitable

This employs the "affirmations" principle. **"I am succeeding"** it is an affirmation that creates a positive environment in which success is more likely.

8. Avoid negative people

You can't afford them. They destroy your creativity and optimism. There is a rule that states it takes 10 optimists longer to lift up one pessimist, than it takes for one pessimist to demoralise 10 optimists!

9. Don't criticise, condemn or complain

Noone ever erected a monument to a critic. Avoid destroying people with the three "C"'s.

10. Smile!

A disarming habit that works! Smile first, the other person usually has to respond.

50.

Give to Receive

"Whatsoever a man soweth, that shall he also reap"
Galatians ch 6 v 7

An absolute confidence in yourself allows you to be generous with other people. When you deal with people, are **you** a **radiator** or a **drain**?

Do you genuinely see how you can help them, or are you only concerned with what you can get from them that will benefit **you**?

To succeed, you **must** be prepared to give to others and to exceed their expectations. If you do, it will be returned to you multiplied many times in value. Give first, then you'll receive.

51.

Opportunity

"A golden opportunity is often disguised as an impossible situation"
Dee Harvard

Opportunity is like a railway train at a station. If you don't get on board, it pulls out without you.

52.

Work, Theory X and Theory Y

"There is no duty we do so much underrate as the duty of being happy"
RL Stevenson

Theory "X" says people love to work and are highly motivated to work, and Theory "Y" says people hate work and will avoid it at all costs.

If you are not striving to achieve your own goals, Theory "Y" could well be right but if you are working for the things you really want, Theory "X" is correct.

No one working for the things they truly want in life finds their work negative.

Completing any task that gets you nearer your goals is always fulfilling.

89

53.

Work, Effort and the Rewards

"The only limit to our realisation of tomorrow will be our doubts of today". Anon.

The first horse in the race sometimes wins by just a nose yet will win its owner five times the prize the second horse wins its owner. Five times the prize sometimes for being just a nose ahead.

Question. Did the horse run five times as fast? No. It was just that bit better focused.

We don't have to run five times faster to accomplish five times as much.

We don't have to run five times faster but we have to be:

1.   **Motivated**
2.   **Focused, or goal orientated**
3.   **Aware of the actions needed to accomplish our goal**
4.   **Prepared to take part**
5.   **Committed to a positive outcome**

If we do, if we don't quit, we will **win!**

part five
summary

Insights gained

_____
_____
_____
_____
_____

Questions to ask

_____
_____
_____
_____
_____

Actions to take

_____
_____
_____
_____
_____

part six

Goals

54.

Inventing Your Own Future

"The future is there for those who invent it".

Fact 1. Every man is a self-made man, only the successful ones admit it.

Fact 2. We either work for an inventor or become one ourselves.

In most free world countries, 95% of the population work for the other 5%. We either work for an inventor, one of the 95%, or become an inventor, one of the 5%.

$\frac{m}{k}$

The future is there for us to invent for ourselves, and we have the right to choose what we want and how we are going to get it.

If we don't, we have to accept that we work for someone else and that they are renting our brains, our creativity and our potential for their own purposes.

How long do **you** want to do that for ?

95

If inventing your own future seems like hard work, remember there is only one alternative, that is for someone to use your potential whilst you are employed by them, helping them invent their future instead of yours.

There is no grey area. It's black and white. Where do you stand right now? Is it possible to invent your own future right now? If not, change something.

55.

Goals

"You set the goal and then you see, you do not see then set the goal"
Louis Tice

To go somewhere, we must know where somewhere is!

We wouldn't fly with a pilot who didn't have a destination. We wouldn't play a game of football without goal posts on the field. Equally, for personal achievement to work we must have specific destinations; meaningful objectives to achieve. This process is known as "goal setting,"

We set goals in the six areas of our lives:

financial
business
private
social
physical
spiritual

The good news about setting and achieving goals is that we are **all** goal orientated and we have a built in goal setting mechanism.

Without consciously selecting any meaningful goals, we nevertheless go through our lives achieving them. Maslow, in his Theory of Hierarchical Needs, states that we strive automatically to fulfil five principle goals. These are the physiological, security, social, esteem, and self-fulfilment goals. All of us are able to achieve most of these needs because our mind has a built in goal seeking mechanism in which the conscious and subconscious minds combine to achieve our goals for us.

The conscious mind gives the instructions to the subconscious mind, and the subconscious mind seeks to carry them out. Whatever the conscious mind asks of it, the subconscious seeks to achieve.

Remember the example we quoted earlier of how this works.

The conscious mind passes the instructions, the subconscious seeks to carry them out.

If the hypnotist puts a subject under hypnosis he can then control their conscious mind and make the subject do all manner of things.

For example, he can indicate to somebody that he is going to place a red hot poker on the palm of the subject's hand. He will then take a pen or pencil, not a red hot poker, place it on the palm of the subject's hand and the subject will react as though the pen or pencil was a red hot poker. This works to such an extent that the skin could even blister.

The conscious mind reacts to the conditions it has been told exist by the hypnotist and passes the facts, about the red hot poker, directly to the subconscious mind which in turn seeks to fulfil the conditions consistent with a red hot poker being placed on the palm of the hand.

Because the subconscious thinks there **is** a red hot poker touching the palm of the hand, it seeks to fulfil the conditions it has been told exist.

We operate on our belief of the facts and not the facts themselves

The human brain is a massive computer. Different programmes inserted into the brain will produce different outcomes.

We can programme our minds to accomplish whatever we truly want.

With the conscious mind controlled by the hypnotist, the subconscious mind seeks to fulfil whatever the conscious mind **believes** it should be achieving in that situation. (Remember the bear, earlier in the book? Was it really a bear or a man dressed as a bear?)

We are all achieving some of our goals now, most of the lower order Maslow goals are achieved by most people every day, because our computer, our brain, is intuitively programmed to do so. But most people do not consciously or deliberately programme their minds to achieve anything meaningful, so achieve nothing meaningful. They do not seek the self-fulfilment they truly desire because they don't know it's available to them.

Our brain is a computer and unless it is programmed to achieve new goals, will keep on achieving the old ones, re-running the old programmes like breathing, eating and sleeping, dressing appropriately, getting to the office on time, and so on. All perfectly acceptable, but not exactly exciting or fulfilling.

Part of the problem is that it is difficult for people to "breakout" and do the unusual. The "social" cost of not conforming with their peer group's expectations of them, is high.

Some people do break these "social" rules but most people would rather stay within their peer groups, rather than stand apart from them.

99

Yet it is precisely that which they have to do, to set goals, to reach for the unusual, to dare to win.

Goal setters and achievers **cannot** be part of the crowd and stand out from the crowd at the same time. Deciding what you want for yourself requires selfishness.

If you want to achieve the things you deep down really want to achieve, you have to choose to act for yourself. Step out from the majority, remembering that most of the majority, sadly, never achieve anything meaningful.

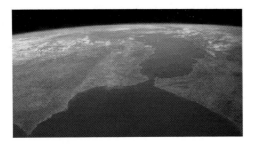

56.

Why Goal Setting Works

"Goals create focus".

We already achieve simple goals each day. If we substitute goals for the mundane ones, the mind will set about accomplishing them.

When we decide on something we'd really like, the mind acts as a magnet, attracting to it all the components necessary to accomplish the goal. This is easily demonstrated.

When you want to buy a new car, the newspapers are full of cars for sale, and you select one. When you don't want to buy a car the newspapers are still full of cars but you don't notice them because they are no longer important to you.

It is only when we set the goal that the information relevant to achieving it becomes more prominent.

Put another way, we set the goal and then we see, we do not see then set the goal.

The mind acts like a tape recorder, it is recording all we experience and how we feel about it. Yet our conscious mind cannot consciously cope with all the information it is being bombarded with, so it filters out what it doesn't need, leaving it to focus on only what it needs to achieve the goal.

When we set a goal we trigger a valuable information filter in the brain. In flying, this system used to be known as a C.A.G. (Central Attention Getter). Our goal is a Central Attention Getter drawing to it the components necessary to achieve it. The brain begins to relate the normally unrelated, and things start to happen.

Because the brain filters out what is not important, it's the value of the information, not the amount that matters.

We must write down our goals and get them sharply focused, the clearer our picture, the more certain the possibility of our achieving it.

57.

Goal Setting Works

"Anything the mind of man can conceive and believe it can achieve"
Napoleon Hill

In a survey of students leaving their university in the U.S.A. in the 60's, they were asked if they had set any goals for their future. The survey showed that only 7% of them had their goals clearly written down.

Twenty years later, the same students were surveyed again and the 7% who had their goals clearly written down had achieved more in terms of wealth and success than the remaining 93%.

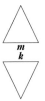

The Proof

Suppose that John is a sales manager and Jim is a salesman. If I am a redundant salesman with money in the bank, John might consider recruiting me because he wants a salesman.

Jim, on the other hand, would want to sell me a product because he only sells products.

John's goal, to recruit, is different from Jim's goal, to sell. I have a different value to John than I do to Jim, because John's goal is different from Jim's.

If Jim didn't have a goal to recruit. I would be of no value to him.

It is his goal that gives me a value.

You set the goal and then you see. You don't see then set the goal.

103

58.

Logic and Succeeding

"Anything's possible" Anon.

Logic says that if we want to achieve twice as much in life we have to try twice as hard, work twice as hard, do twice as much.

It is not true. We can achieve **extraordinary** increases in our productivity, and our success in life, **without** having to make an **extraordinary** effort.

$$\frac{m}{k}$$

We do not have to work five times harder to achieve five times as much. We can achieve exceptional improvements in our success rate without extraordinary increases in effort.

59.

Logic and Goal Setting

"Big goals create a fear of failure, a lack of goals guarantees it".

We can achieve five to ten times the success we have achieved to date, if we commit ourselves to our goals.

To do this, logic dictates that the sequence we have to follow is:

1, 2,3,4, etc, ...

Well, it is **logical**, but in goal achieving terms, **it's not true.**

With clearly set goals the exceptional focus that results creates exponential results: **1, 3, 9, 27,** not **1, 2, 3, 4.** You can leap-frog forward, missing steps in between, and accelerate your results without visiting every number logically in sequence.

Is this making sense? If we set the goal and believe its achieveable, we can leap over entire conventional logical processes and achieve our goals, without waiting in line to go through each step one at a time.

60.

Current Reality and our Future Dream

"Strong lives are motivated by dynamic purposes".

We must be so committed to achieving our goal that we see it as a virtual reality in our minds.

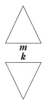

Our future dream has to be so clearly defined and so strongly desired that we cannot tolerate the current reality of our circumstances.

We have to want our future dream more than our current reality.

61.

Personal Principles

"There are three necessities in life to be happy ....a valued identity, belief and value in what we do, and love" Samuel J Leon

Whatever our personal beliefs, we set out to live our lives in a manner consistent with principles based on those beliefs.

Our own views on right and wrong, morality, work, money and ethics all identify with these basic beliefs that we have.

We should list these beliefs so that they act as signposts for our consistent behaviour and to ensure that they prevail throughout our life.

It is impossible to attract and keep that which we do not deep down believe we truly deserve or are entitled to have. It is not possible to set goals and achieve them without confirming that what we seek is consistent with our code of conduct, our personal beliefs.

Listing those beliefs we hold true, forms part of the goal setting process. You will find pages in the work section· of your goal setting book to complete this list.

Typical statements might be:

1. Treat all people fairly
2. Avoid excesses
3. Maintain a positive attitude
4. Be courteous to others

Your list will lengthen as you become more used to setting and resetting your goals and will act as a reminder of your deeply held beliefs.

62.

Setting Goals – How?

"Make no little plans: they have no magic to stir mens' souls"
Daniel Burnham

We set goals in the six main areas of our lives:

Financial
Business
Social
Private
Physical
Spiritual

What exactly are your goals?

This is your opportunity to dream. You are going to require privacy, peace and quiet, plain paper and a pen and at least a couple of hours to yourself.

1.   Write them all down

Having arranged this, write down everything you'd really like to have, be, or achieve in life.

For example:

- to own a large detached house with 3 acres of ground
- to play tennis well
- to be more patient
- to have £100,000 in savings
- to travel around the world
- to be a good after dinner speaker

The list is as long as your imagination allows it!

Two Rules

When you write your goals down, follow two basic rules..........

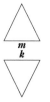

1. Your goals are the things that you want.

Don't change them to conform with what you believe others might expect of you.

2. Don't leave anything out.

Anything you'd like should be written down. Don't prejudge your ability to accomplish it. Write it down no matter how impossible it may seem at the time. Leave nothing out.

Five life changing questions.

Ask yourself the following questions that I first heard Brian Tracy use, to get you to focus on what really counts

- a. **If you had 10 minutes to live, who would you call and what would you say?**
- b. **If you had six months to live, how would you spend your time?**
- c. **What five things do you value most in your life ?**
- d. **What are the three most important goals in your life right now?**
- e. **What one thing would you attempt to do, if you knew you wouldn't fail?**

3. Define each goal in detail

Write each goal in specific terms. Expand each goal to include a detailed and precise description of what you seek.

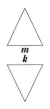

For example: A large detached house with 3 acres of ground becomes:

A large detached house with 3 acres in the country within 30 minutes journey time from the office. 3 reception rooms, 2 bathrooms, 4 bedrooms, study, 2 garages, kitchen, utility room, outbuildings to include a greenhouse and 2 stables.

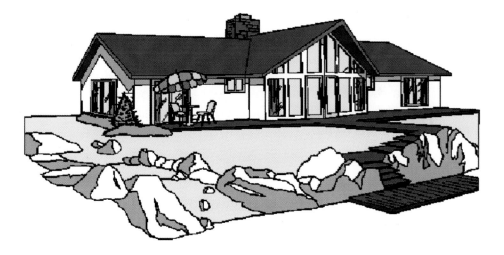

For example:
To play tennis well becomes:

To be able to play competently at club level in both singles and doubles, to have had two dozen lessons, and to have got to the last sixteen in the club league.

These goals are **specific** not generalised.

4. Detail

The added detail helps you visualise the goal more clearly. The more you define it, the clearer it becomes. The clearer it becomes, the greater the likelihood you have of accomplishing it.

5. Priorities

Put each of the six goals listed in order of priority. Don't be concerned if some goals appear on more than one list, it happens.

6. Deadlines

A goal is meaningless without a deadline. The first goal on each list should have a deadline for accomplishment and if you have never really set goals before, that deadline should be no less than 2 months and no more than 6 months away.

7. Plan of Action

Take the first goal from each list and write down the actions that you think you will have to take to achieve it.

8. Obstacles

Write down all the obstacles that will prevent your goal being attained , then write down solutions in terms of the attitudes and actions you will have to adopt to overcome them.

Here is an example:

Physical Goal   Weight 12 stone 7 lbs by September 1st
Present weight: 13 stone 9 lbs

Actions
Exercise - run or walk 2 miles 5 times a week
Diet - avoid butter, fatty meats, cheese
Weight loss - 8 weeks at 2 lbs a week

9. Affirmations state the goal in the present tense

If you state the goal in the present tense, it enters the subconscious from the conscious as though already achieved. This is deliberate. It makes the subconscious behave as if the goal is already attained, ensuring it behaves in a manner consistent with its accomplishment.

This "trick" of the mind gets the subconscious working on bringing about the change you desire. It brings the goal nearer, faster. You are conditioning your mind, **programming** your mind, to believe that the goal is achieved. This creation of a false belief in the subconscious creates the correct conditions for the subconscious mind to be in step with your conscious desire to attain the goal.

Use of present tense affirmations to reinforce your goal, i.e. **"I am punctual", "I am enthusiastic", "I am successful",** programmes the subconscious.

10. Actions

Carry out the steps of your action plan in the complete faith that they will come about. Remember winners have belief without evidence.

63.

Affirmations

"To be all that we can be, not just who we are" John Denver

Your **Definite Chief Aim**. Once all the goals are set a specific pattern will emerge and a definite chief aim relating to your life, probably some five to ten years hence, will emerge.

Your **Definite Chief Aim** becomes the dominating drive for your five to ten year business plan and all your goals are subordinated to it and co-ordinated with it.

Your **Definite Chief Aim** is your specific purpose for the next five to ten years, it will give you the long term perspective necessary to overcome the short-term red traffic light obstacles that will inevitably occur.

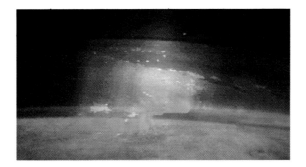

64.

Goal Lists and Affirmations

"Goal setting is important, goal doing is more important".

Your goal list will look something like this:

My Personal Goals

1. **Weight 12 stone 7 lbs by 1.9.98**

2. **To be more decisive in my business**

3. **To save £2,500 by Christmas 1998**

4. **To start work on my family tree this year**

5. **To earn promotion in my job by January 1999**

6. **To take six golf lessons by November 1st, 1998**

Signed: A Chiever   1.4.1998

Your affirmations for these goals will look like this :

Affirmations

1. **I am 12 stone 7 lbs**

2. **I am decisive**

3. **I am saving £2,500 and will have it set aside by Christmas**

4. **I am drawing up my family tree**

65.

Using Your Goal Lists and Affirmations

"One day is worth two tomorrow's, never leave that 'til tomorrow which you can do today" Benjamin Franklin

To continually keep your goals in the forefront of your mind, you must keep copies of them, handwritten each time, dated and signed by you, where you will continually see them. For example, copies should be:

- In your wallet
- In your diary
- On your steering wheel
- On your bathroom mirror
- On your desk

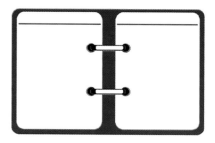

These will act as a reinforcement each time you see them.

66.

Pictures

*"Man's desires are limited by his perceptions,
none can desire what he has not perceived"* William Blake

**The more clearly we see our goals, the more likely we are to
achieve them. To make them "live" once you've set them, use
pictures prominently displayed on your desk, in your study, in
your diary, on your bedroom mirror to remind you of why you
are striving to achieve your goals.**

Get detailed pictures of your goals and surround yourself with them.
The power of these pictures will reinforce your ability to achieve your
goals. Visualise in your mind your circumstances when you've achieved
your goal.

Take time to build a mental picture of the way life will be and how you'll
feel when your goal is attained.

Picture your goals as though they were in your **possession** already.
Visualisation makes your goals come to life.

67.

Rewards

"Destiny is not a matter of chance, it is a matter of choice".

Aside from the satisfaction of achieving the goal itself, give yourself a reward for attaining the goal, a dinner, a weekend away, an item you've always wanted, or a gift for your spouse, something that will be a reminder of its achievement.

Cross your goal off the list, keep the original written statement of the goal and write across it in bold **"ACHIEVED"** and then put the goal statement into your "Goals Achieved" portfolio.

Keep your goal setting information in an A4 binder with plastic sleeves, or a presentation portfolio. The internal layout should be:

1. **Definitive Chief Aim**
2. **Total Goal List**
3. **Financial Goals**
4. **Business Goals**
5. **Physical Goals**
6. **Private Goals**
7. **Social Goals**
8. **Spiritual Goals**
9. **Affirmations and Belief Statements**
10. **Previous Goals Achieved**
11. **Previous Goal Lists.**

This record of your goal setting is the most important personal document you will ever own. It serves to remind you of what you have decided to do and will have achieved.

68.

Focus

"Circumstances what circumstances ? I make circumstances"
Napoleon Bonaparte

Napoleon achieved historic battle victories with smaller numbers of soldiers than his enemies. Their efforts were concentrated in small areas and their individual successes led to the greater victory being accomplished.

As a boy, I remember using a magnifying glass to focus the sun's rays on one small point creating intense heat. The sun could beat down all day and wouldn't start a fire but a simple magnifying glass focusing the sun's energy on to a piece of paper, can do so in a few seconds.

A camera without a focus produces at best a hazy picture but with focus can create award winning images.

A hazy goal is likely at best to produce a hazy result. Refine and define your goal so that it is clearly focused. The apparently impossible can be accomplished if your goal is focused sharply.

69.

Can Goal Setting Work?

"Aim high. There is plenty of room."
Donald G Reynolds

Goal setting **doesn't** work if the following points are true:

1. People without goals and with no plans for their future still get everything they want from life.

2. A person's level of desire has no effect on their chances of success.

3. We don't dream.

4. Human potential is limited to what we know it can achieve now.

5. We cannot expand our capacity to achieve more.

6. To win a prize twice as large as the person who comes second, a winner has to be twice as good as the person who comes second.

7. The most successful people in life are those with the most academic qualifications.

8. People who work as employees for other people succeed the most in life.

Goal setting **does** work if:

1. **People with clearly defined goals achieve more than people without them.**

2. **A burning desire to succeed has a direct effect on our chances of success.**

Clearly goal setting works

70.

The Shortest Distance Between Two Points

"A goal is a dream with a deadline"
John F Savage

The shortest distance between two points is a straight line.

Setting a goal with a deadline, is a straight line.

Set goals, they get you to your desired destination in the shortest time possible, giving you more time to pursue the next one, or to rest after your achievement.

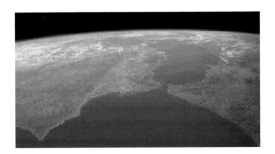

part six
summary

Insights gained

_____

_____

_____

_____

_____

Questions to ask

_____

_____

_____

_____

_____

Actions to take

_____

_____

_____

_____

_____

part seven

Maintaining Our Momentum

71.

Success

*"You can get anything in life you want,
if you'll help others get what they want"* Zig Ziglar

Success is a journey, not a destination. We never arrive.

Our purpose is to extend our potential by striving to succeed. Setting goals gives us direction and desire, when expressed as motivation, gives us our drive. We go as far as we can and then we see further. Our goal setting horizons are like the earth. When we arrive at the horizon, there's a new one to move towards.

As we go forward, our horizon is reset. Success is out there on the horizon and as we strive, our horizon changes. We see further and set new goals, reach new horizons, progress further.

As we achieve more we go further, the further we go, the further we can see. We should set **high goals** and strive to be as great as we can now be. Our potential to succeed is far greater than we realise. We have an unlimited capacity to achieve and there are opportunities constantly waiting to be achieved.

72.

We Become What We Think About

"We are what we believe we are" Benjamin N Cardozo

The principle of affirmations, of "assuming a virtue we do not have," confirms that if we implant an idea sufficiently strongly in our minds we can bring it to pass.

If we want to be more enthusiastic, for example, we say:

"I am enthusiastic"
"I am enthusiastic"
"I am enthusiastic"

and the subconscious creates the conditions for it to occur.

If we pass no specific messages to our subconscious, our current thoughts will still engage us in conversation and we will become what we think about.

We have to feed positive "Yes I Can" messages into our subconscious and actively avoid the negative messages.

73.

Time Management

"Time is slipping underneath our feet" Edward Fitzgerald

Do we value time? An outstanding senior executive from my father's franchise company made me realise the value of time. I was 29 at the time and working for his company. He asked me when I wanted to retire, and I replied age 65. He then asked me how I felt with only 8.21 years to retirement. "But I've got 36 years of work before I retire", I said. His reply was to change the course of my life.

He explained that if I worked **40** hours a week for **50** weeks a year, I had **2000** hours available each year for the remaining **36** years of my working life before I reached 65. That was **72,000** hours, or **3000** days. Divided by **365** days that was just **8.21** working years.

He went on to explain that an extra 30 minutes a day, six days a week, would give me virtually a whole extra working month a year. I determined then not to waste time while I still had goals to achieve.

132

74.

Goal Achieving – Tension Relieving

"Time is like a river" Marcus Aurelius Antonius

Time is only spent in one of two ways. Goal Achieving, or Tension Relieving. We choose which way we use it.

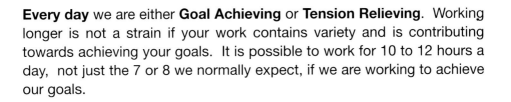

Every day we are either **Goal Achieving** or **Tension Relieving**. Working longer is not a strain if your work contains variety and is contributing towards achieving your goals. It is possible to work for 10 to 12 hours a day, not just the 7 or 8 we normally expect, if we are working to achieve our goals.

75.

Urgent Versus Important

"I sometimes like to measure a man by the things he decides to leave undone. The man who insists on getting 100% of his job done either doesn't have enough to do or doesn't have the kind of stuff it takes to succeed in business today"
Herman Krannert, "The Timewasters"

Which do you do first? The urgent or the important? If it's urgent and important it comes first. If it's important but not urgent it comes second.

But if it's urgent but not important it also comes **first**.

So how do we overcome the tyranny of the urgent ?

1. List all our tasks.
2. Put them in order of their importance.
3. Do the first one first, the second one second and carry on until finished.

Whatever is left undone is less important than those that have been done, so all that can be done has been done.

And what about the urgent? Just leave an hour a day "urgent" slot for the unexpected.

76.

The Effective Use of Time for Goal Achieving

"Not having a goal is more dangerous than not reaching it" Rick Thomas.

Most people's use of time!

Most people in employment typically work 48 weeks per year and take 8 days in public holidays. Starting from 365 days, less 104 days for weekends, 20 weekdays for holidays and 8 public holidays, this leaves 233 working days, each day containing 7.5 hours of work, a total of 1,747.5 hours a year.

How much time, including holidays, do they actually have available?
365 days of which 7 hours a day are spent asleep; 17 hours a day are spent awake giving a total of 6,205 hours in a year.

$$\frac{1747.5}{6205} \quad \text{or } \textbf{28\%}$$

They use only 28% of their waking life to make a living, not a life time!

The Goal Setters Use of Time

Goals are set in the six principle areas of our life:

Financial
Business
Social
Private
Physical
Spiritual

Goal achievers will pursue their goals typically for six days a week, with one day for rest using 10 hours of each day to achieve their goals.

The time available for goal achievers could therefore be (assuming 48 weeks work a year and 8 Public Holidays), starting with 52 weeks of six days a week, 312 days, less 4 weeks holiday and 8 public holidays, leaves 280 days. At 10 hours a day this gives goal achievers 2,800 hours in a year, out of an available total of 6,205 hours. Most goal achievers therefore have

$$\frac{2800}{6205} \quad \text{or } \mathbf{45\%}$$

of their waking life, at least, to achieve their goals.

136

Which one wins ?

Which of the two below do you think stands more chance of success?

Employee   **Goal Achiever**

1747.5 hours   **2800 hours**

The goal achiever has **60.22%** more time **and** is more committed
to his goals.

If these figures make us uncomfortable, it is because "most people" fit
the first category.
With a set of clearly written goals, is it any wonder that the 7% who set
goals   in the survey of North American college students,   had
accomplished more after 20 years than the 93% who had not?

Focused use of time achieves goals.

77.

Delegation

"Extends results from what a man can do to what a man can control"
Dr. R Alec MacKenzie, "The Time Trap".

You are your greatest resource. Do you see yourself as such?

What price per hour do you set on your goal achieving time?

"No one does it as well as me" is the excuse we use for not delegating. "I like to know what's going on" is another, "I'm hanging on to these more trivial tasks because I understand them, they don't challenge them, they don't challenge me, but I'm safe while I'm doing them and they are useful, aren't they?" are the reasons why most people don't delegate.

You cannot grow into the areas of your life where you need to grow, if you hang on to the daily clutter of trivial tasks that you feel secure in completing. If you don't have a set of clearly focused personal goals, every task has equal value and relevance. If you do have a set of clearly focused goals, you need time to accomplish them and you will still obtain the key facts to ensure you have the relevant information to keep control.

Personal growth comes from taking on the roles that help you grow. However, "letting go" and "letting others see the rabbit" is all part of a clearly focused mind.

Delegate, it frees you up to be more creative! It gives you the space to multiply your results. It lets you act on those things that truly change your future.

Objections to delegating

Objection: *The people I delegate to don't do it as well as I do.*

Answer: Oh yes they do, it is often the case that the person you delegate to does it **better** than you.

Objection: *I like to know everything.*

Answer: Knowing everything isn't the key to staying in control. In the end you are overloaded. What matters is distinguishing between the **valuable** and the rest. Delegate and ask only to be fed back the key facts of a situation.

You are still in charge but no longer cluttered up with the trivia. $\frac{m}{k}$

139

78.

Persistence

"Never, never, never give up" Winston Churchill

Persist. Quitters never win, winners never quit.

Setting goals is one thing. Persisting in their pursuit is entirely another. We have to be prepared to try and try and try **and** try, to achieve the things we really want from life.

If the pain of getting exceeds the hurt of wanting, then it is not a goal, it's a want.

Decide which of your goals you deep down truly desire and don't give up on striving to attain those goals.

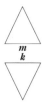 **You cannot fail unless you've quit.**

79.

Practice

"Failure is the opportunity to begin again more intelligently" Henry Ford

Practice, practice, practice

You will be disappointed. You will fail. You will be discouraged **but** gradually, as you try and try again, it gets easier and success becomes more predictable.

When faced with failure, say **"yes, I can"** and press on.

80.

Winners

"Winners have belief without evidence whilst the mediocre need evidence on which to base their beliefs"

- Mix with winners
- Avoid the mediocre
- Don't make the same mistake twice
- Seek out those who are better than you and ask how
- Think "how would a winner handle this situation?" and press on towards your goals.

part seven
summary

Insights gained

_____
_____
_____
_____
_____

Questions to ask

_____
_____
_____
_____
_____

Actions to take

_____
_____
_____
_____
_____

part eight

Your Personal Goal Planning Section

PERSONAL GOAL PLANNING

This part of the book is yours. Please use this section of the book to actually invent your future. Photocopy the pages. Record all your dreams, ambitions and wishes. Carry them with you.

It is divided into four parts:

1. The **Dreams and Ambitions** section, **p149-p151**.
    Use these pages, one section at a time to list everything you've ever wanted, this is the first part of goal setting. If you run out of pages, photocopy them, whatever you do, don't stint on **making as long a list as possible** of all your dreams, goals and hopes. Four pages at a time should be long enough to convert your mind's dreams into written statements such as "to own a large house in the country", or "to travel around the world" etc.

2. Six **Goals Lists** sections. Pages on which having written down your life's dreams, you can then set out your refined lists, two pages for each of the goals.
    The six **Goals Lists** are

Financial	**152**
Business	**154**
Social	**156**
Private	**158**
Spiritual	**160**
Physical	**162**

    Fill out the first six pages after you have completed your first goal setting exercise, and use the next section when you need to revise your goals, usually annually, and copy the pages for extended use beyond your first six goal setting sessions.

3. **The third section contains pages, p164 and 165, for listing your goals and affirmations. Carry with you. Photocopy the pages for this purpose.**

4. This section contains eight **Goals with Deadlines** pages. Again they can be photocopied allowing you to list your goals for:

one month	166
three months	167
six months	168
twelve months	169
three years	170
five years	171
ten years	172
unspecified time	173

5. This section allows you to enter extra **"Laws of Success and Wisdom Acquired"** since reading this book. It consists of pages headed

"LAWS OF SUCCESS AND WISDOM ACQUIRED".

DREAMS, AMBITIONS AND WISHES LISTS

Leave **nothing** out , write down what **you** want, don't change it to please other people. No-one will ever read this list except you.

Name .... Date ....

DREAMS, AMBITIONS AND WISHES LISTS

Leave **nothing** out , write down what **you** want, don't change it to please other people. No-one will ever read this list except you.

Name .... Date ....

DREAMS, AMBITIONS AND WISHES LISTS

Leave **nothing** out , write down what **you** want, don't change it to please other people. No-one will ever read this list except you.

Name .... Date ....

FINANCIAL GOALS

Name .... Date ....

FINANCIAL GOALS

Name .... Date ....

BUSINESS GOALS

Name .... Date ....

BUSINESS GOALS

Name .... Date ....

SOCIAL GOALS

Name .... Date ....

SOCIAL GOALS

Name .... Date ....

PRIVATE GOALS

Name .... Date ....

PRIVATE GOALS

Name .... Date ....

SPIRITUAL GOALS

Name .... Date ....

SPIRITUAL GOALS

Name .... Date ....

PHYSICAL GOALS

Name .... Date ....

PHYSICAL GOALS

Name .... Date ....

GOALS

AFFIRMATIONS

MY PERSONAL GOALS FOR 1 MONTH

These will be accomplished by ....

MY PERSONAL GOALS FOR 3 MONTHS

These will be accomplished by ....

MY PERSONAL GOALS FOR 6 MONTHS

These will be accomplished by ....

MY PERSONAL GOALS FOR 1 YEAR

These will be accomplished by ....

MY PERSONAL GOALS FOR 3 YEARS

These will be accomplished by ....

MY PERSONAL GOALS FOR 5 YEARS

These will be accomplished by ....

171

MY PERSONAL GOALS FOR 10 YEARS

These will be accomplished by ....

172

MY PERSONAL GOALS FOR _____

These will be accomplished by ....

LAWS OF SUCCESS AND WISDOM ACQUIRED

part nine

Lessons Learned

These pages are for you to record your own opinions and beliefs on. Write down all truths that come to you as you pursue your goal setting ....